THE CHAMELEON

THE CHAMELEON

POEMS

RITA SIGNORELLI-PAPPAS

The Chameleon, poems
Copyright © 2025 Rita Signorelli-Pappas
First Edition

All rights reserved. No part of this book may be reproduced or transmitted in any form or by any means, electronic, digital, or mechanical, including photocopy, audio recording, or any information storage and retrieval system, without prior permission from the publisher or author (except by reviewers who may quote brief passages).

Cover art by Jacob Arms

Published by Serving House Books
Lawrence Landing Company
Raleigh, North Carolina 27609
United States of America

www.servinghousebooks.com

Serving House Books is a proud member of

Independent Book Publishers Association
 and
Community of Literary Magazines and Presses

Paperback ISBN: 978-1-947175-67-9

Library of Congress Control Number: 2025930739

SERVING HOUSE BOOKS

ACKNOWLEDGMENTS

Grateful acknowledgment is made to the editors of the following magazines in which these poems, sometimes in different form, first appeared:

Claudel Studies:
"Asylum Journal: The Internment of Camille Claudel"
The Cresset: "Harem" "Magdalene"
Crosscurrents: "Daybook: Leonard Woolf"
Cumberland Poetry Review:
"Swans" and "Face in the Glass"
Interim: "A Child's Blindness"
The Literary Review: "Bacchus Sees Ariadne"
The Midwest Quarterly: "Themes of Initiation"
Poet Lore: "Shelley's Heart"
San Jose Studies: "Fasting Woman"
Serving House Journal: "The Chameleon"
Southern Humanities Review: "Sunflowers"
The Women's Review of Books:
"Memoir: Phillipa Chaucer"

For René Steinke and Richard Wertime

CONTENTS

The Chameleon	1
The Plague Artist	2
The Polish Poet	3
Fasting Woman	4
Sunflowers	5
Emma Bovary's Daughter	6
Themes of Initiation	7
Face in the Glass	9
Love in the Halocene	10
The Mother	11
Boy of the Violets	12
Harem	13
Asylum Journal...	14
Katydid	16
The Family Plot	17
Harlequinade	18
Cicadas	19
Eve	20
In Hospice	22
The House Ghosts Speak	23
A Child's Blindness	24
Sebastian	25
The Apparition Comes	26
Anonymous Woman	27
Wind	28
Swans	29
Kindness	30
Icicles	31
Mask	32
Winter Walk	33
Lot's Wife	34

Magdalene	35
The Waiting	36
Interview with Mary	37
Pilgrim Journey	38
Bacchus Sees Ariadne	39
Daphne Afterward	40
Memoir: Philippa Chaucer	41
Ophelia	42
Shelley's Heart	43
Piranesi at the Tomb of...	44
The Old World	45
Daybook: Leonard Woolf	46
Oliver in Sutri	48
Jonah	49
Thoreau	50
Dear Natalia	51
Self-portrait	52

The Chameleon

It's easy to forget her
with the nerve endings
of a rainbow and glands
like elegant rosettes

especially if the blue
door of darkness opens
and catastrophe just stands there
snapping a salute

but then I remember
Hamlet grinning and eating
from her dish as if
he could finally feel

the bright oils of her goodness
rinsing his bones like
a soft stream—and I remember
her green lungs filling with euphoria,

her long tongue leaping
the length of her body
like a ribbon of brocade
to snag a day-flying moth.

Then her quick toes begin to curl
and I remember to grip life's pain
like a branch flung over
an abyss—I remember

the excited lunge of imagination—
my own wild hunger
rushing to seize
winged promises in the air

The Plague Artist

Why were the clouds racing overhead
when it was almost dark, why
did the lines tilt and go sliding
toward the paper's edge, why
had the cross-hatching thinned?

From the beginning she has learned
to let her gaze go deep into
the turning panoramic dream
of this city that never knew
it could be broken.

In the windy twilight she inhales,
tasting ash, smelling pine.
Plague has emptied the streets
but the birds still breathe and fly,
the lines contract and expand.

In quarantine her soul stays
locked in flame and ice,
her forehead bowed, her fingers
moving to the rhythmic rush of clouds
that surround and steady her.

The Polish Poet

Like a shaman or a dancer
balanced on a rope
he bowed and took my hand
as if we were alone together
inside the crowded room.

He wore one black glove
and his gaze kept drifting
out into the Chicago night
as if he were slowly coasting
into a port of dream.

He told me that his wife
was a dramatical woman
and when it was time to leave
he paused to kiss my hand as if
I were a woman of her intensity.

Fasting Woman

Every morning when my eyes open
I feel my throat slide shut again.
I dream of live Byzantine statues
descending from marble pedestals
like angels swinging their censers—
they keep singing because
they want me to be their queen.

Each time the strangeness
tries to swallow me, you come
and raise a cup of honey to my mouth,
but how can I comply, how can I leave
this cruel, hypnotic paradise,
this wizard's dream in which
the cool abstract lines of my body
speak only of salvation?

I am one of the bad ones—
doomed, giddy, lovesick—
that your amazement circles
like a blinded dove
while I walk this borderland
more ghost than woman
head sequined with willow straw.

Sunflowers

Blind as the ghost of Oedipus
they lean on tremoring arms
of autumn wind.

I find it hard not to stare
at such saintliness, that stooped
and holy way they learn to die,
the suddenly daring sway
of their silver backbones
through shimmering light.

I want to walk this windblown garden
as flocks of dazzled starlings
cloud the shipwrecked day,
as the sunflowers' gilded spines
click and dance again.

I want to live fated and free,
my soul woven into the spell
of a cicada's song.
I want to partner that dying row
of sunflowers and face
the passion of those fiery heads.

                        For Richard Maxwell

Emma Bovary's Daughter

At night your face floats out at me
from the mirror as you anoint me
with the dust of granite moons.

Mother, sleep cannot swallow your constancy.
At dawn you return to settle behind my brow
and enter the pulse points at my wrists.

I bite my pomegranate lips but there is
no end to the redness. The print
of your crimson mouth is on everything.

I watch the sun clot into a valentine
of ash as your fine invisible endless
snow keeps whitening me.

I heard the click years ago when you
first plotted my surrender, snapped
your wintry purse shut on my soul.

Themes of Initiation

I had heard that he was a poet,
but his sullen lips bulged
and his heavy-lidded eyes rolled—
he had jowls that trembled whenever

he laughed or told his crude jokes.
When he shook my hand and happened to see
the band of gold, he winked and asked,
"Is this the ring from *The Story of O?*"

I withdrew my hand, imagining
his death drop down a canyon in Utah.
But twenty years later I began to read his poems,
the lines so singular and bold

that the breath caught in my throat.
I slept and dreamed
I was in a French chateau dressed
like an owl, that two masked men

called me into the bedchamber
where a fire blazed, that they
thrust me back naked over a chair,
then lifted me like a fish.

I woke with arms flung back over my head
and wrists locked together—the sound
rising through my mouth was not
a song but a cry of pain

and I entered the river of daylight
while wind soothed the reeds on shore
like a bow easing the loneliness
of a violin. I began to sing

the poet's words over the over—
I saw the strange and stunning
body of Osiris in its sacred coffin
floating in a rapture of secrecy

over the clear, sunlit waves.
My body began to shake, I started
casting my net into the water
for the vanished bones. I was patient.

I waited until I had found almost all of him.
Then I lay in the shade of a tall sycamore,
a woman with the shadow of a ram.
I kept thinking about

the poet's best self tensed into his ugly
and beautiful hands as they pulled
down a branch to whittle what was missed—
the sweet, the blissful brow of Osiris.

There was a wonderful strength now in my body.
I wanted to dance the fandango,
the sky was suddenly brilliant,
I wanted to fall and rise like a marble column

on the shore of the Nile. I saw how
the crow's head kept glittering into blue,
how the hidden tomb went to leaf
and unlocked all its blossoms of blood.

Face in the Glass

She stares into her mirror
but the looking glass is empty.

She powders her forehead,
paints her full lips scarlet,
darkens the lines of her brows
and looks once again.

Nothing is reflected.

She tries a plumed headdress,
she braids her hair with velvet
and places a rose behind her ear.

Blank. Still blank.

She paints her mouth
more slowly now, she applies
three separate layers of crimson.
Then on her cheek she draws
a beauty spot shaped like a star.

But still no face in the glass.

Now she casts aside her
pencils, powders, and paints,
her life as *objet d'art*.
She puts a canvas on an easel
and fashions a self
figured like a crescent moon.

The sky goes blank.

She stares into her washbowl
and sees reflected
a scythe of yellow light.

Love in the Halocene

A clairvoyant moon
accompanied us the night
I drove you back
from the city of lagoons.

Rifting was so much
easier than I had guessed—
there was such civility
and not a speck of betrayal.

Your loss that night
simply synchronized
with all the rest
into a spotless balance.

So there were these—
the friend back from Venice,
the suicide in Paris,
the Greek from Kremasti.

That was the tart sum
of love for me
adrift in the Halocene
body soul and heart.

The Mother

I can feel the rose flutter and throb
into bloom like the heart
of a taut, angry mother.

Leathery petals neither sleeping
nor waking quiver and wince,
swell and burn.

Each day I come to look
for the mystically hidden
thorn-lit and leaf-lit buds.

Each day I try to understand
love's wounding—how it took me
all the way down to the roots.

Boy of the Violets

Cradled in violets,
you follow me everywhere
while my pulse
keeps anxious pace
with your every breath.

The clement bees come
to soothe and feed you
under a silk canopy
the dusk threaded
with lavender haze.

Already I've learned how to
hold you without touch.
I've watched the last bee
drift slowly away, heard your
soft cries fade into sleep.

I wake in crimson light
as you rise through
my desperate thoughts.
How you bloom and bloom—
I can almost feel you in my hands!

Harem

In a thin fever he
would choose each one of us.
Then we felt the sky melt
into a queer yellow smoke.

Now memory is only the knitted hat
I tied once under my chin.
And love. . . but who ever
thinks of such things here?

There's a statue of his father
over by the souks—he looks
so frail and mysterious
in his alabaster shoes!

Soon our children will stop smiling.
Their play will cease.
Soon they will disbelieve us—
bright angels of our uneasiness.

Asylum Journal:
The Internment of Camille Claudel

All night your memory passes over my body
like wind ringing glass, Rodin.
The dream burns down to nightmare.
The heart's giddy drumroll
goes blinding into ash.
This is the nightmare: turning
to find the moon is only
a house of broken plaster
and there are shadows of dazed bats
stroking its bare lonely rooms.

Mon petit Paul! He brings me clay,
embraces me, murmuring that the bright
marble bodies of the stars are so pristine
I could be their creator. I begin to see
how easily Paul can bear the shrieks
of these disconsolate creatures.
Paul can save himself, he can
walk away. Can I step through
this bloodlit colonnade of bones
into the simple light of the sun?
Still, he brings me clay.

Rain sweeping against the window
A knock No
The sound of a lock breaking
Then faces
The faces of strangers
brutal floodlit scrubbed
My wrists grabbed and bound
My shut eyes
dissolving pools of fiery blue light

    a shattering
           winding
                  scream

Green undulating twilight.
Naked tango of the trees.
When the ruthless violin pauses
love clutches us in its satin shroud.
This is the nightmare: waking years later
locked in that long hurricane shudder
rushing us body-to-body down to dust.

In the fantasy chapel
a woman facing her altar
to shape her prayer
rubbing it with pumice
or with sand.
In the fantasy chapel
the dazzled hush
of two white hands
endlessly lifting
to mold wet clay.
Always her smooth face flushed
with the swift whirling joy
of this nude instinct for melody.
This fever waltz.

You knew, you knew
how the truth loved me, Rodin.
How its blood-hungry shadow followed me
through the dream's long arcade.
This is the nightmare: my vision
        caged and abandoned
        like a mad dove
        that wept and sang once
        in the wilderness of your hands.

Katydid

How I wanted to touch it
the first morning.

A crisp fixed cut-out
of emerald light.

A repose I had yet to know
greening on my doorsill.

It was not the new house
or the new town—no.

It was that miracle
of perfect stillness.

The quiet joy of a stasis
opening in me.

The Family Plot

Far from the agitation of the trees
the family plot stood square in the rain.
You were all there, every one of you.
Your sister's words no longer stung.
Your brother had stopped his scolding.
Your mother's fears had fled for good.

Now you all lay stitched and knotted
in the woven shawl of eternity.
And no more one of you, I was only
a giddy pebble kicked up by rain
that came spinning crazily through
the fenced, straight-edged swath of earth.

Harlequinade

If I rubbed cinders on my forehead
in the shape of a raptor's claw.
Sharpened my egg tooth. Pulled off my shoes.
Thrust the faded boa of a dream-wise
night over my shoulders.
Under waving branches. Graying sky.

Left my dazed ghosts to spin and play
somewhere in the mountain forest.
Peeled the apples. Tuned a rusty lute.
Fastened my torn mask to a stick
and gazed out the ragged eye holes
at autumn's ruined carnival.

Than I could leave behind
life's wry tableaus. Ease myself
into the huge and humming dark.
Let my mind melt away in a wave
that rises and rises and rises
before it starts to break.

Cicadas

Beads shaken in a coconut shell.
Electric vibrations of thought.
Whirring chants that refuse to stop.
Agitations of the soul.

While the sky continues to sing.

The heart stays latticed in red and black.
Yet they go silent when they begin
 scaling the walls of my house.

Oh I try to flick them away.
But they stick. And fly into my hair.
You see, they are avid.
They care too much.

This is the poem I meant to compose
the first time they bridged
the fragile moat of my life
under the light of blood moons.

Eve

It was dawn
or it was dusk
when a shadow
spangled like
a tambourine
first uncoiled
and wound its way
down a twisted
willow branch
pulsing a trail
of glowing light—it had
a voice
that slowed
and gentled her
like the memory
of a trance
so she simply
did what it asked
and lifted the bowl
filled with the juice
of fresh apples
all the way up
to her lowered mouth
and she felt
her arm go numb
as another voice
came thundering
through the orchard
and she saw
the serpent's body

writhe and slide away
and her world died
the way the limbs
of a willow slip
beneath the surface
of deep dark water.

In Hospice

During the final day she
came rushing through the door.
Though she had always been there
coiling and uncoiling.

Your body jerked forward
fear widening your eyes
when you cried "Mother!"
I stepped slowly aside.

For hadn't she always
known you better than I?
Wasn't she only reclaiming
what was rightfully hers?

It was a scene of justice—
the corrected imbalance of years.
Death blew its enchanted pipe
and the ophidian reappeared.

The House Ghosts Speak

What do the invisible know?
How to live inside the pause
between breathing in
and breathing out. How to live
in an utterly white world.

What can the invisible do?
They can open themselves
endlessly. They can forbear.
There are no icons. There is
only the suspension of breath.

Where do the invisible go?
They atomize into dust.
They have nothing to hold.
They are blank but not desperate.
They are somewhere beyond craving.

For weeks and months and years
they persevere. They are humble
as they go roaming through
the lightning and the thunder.
Transformed, they do not look back.

A Child's Blindness

I am the drowned darling
you keep trying to charm out
of the water, the hungry
dolphin who leaps smiling
inside your shipwrecked heart.

My eyes touch bandages.
They are stuffed with absence.
But I hear everything, even
the taut breathing of pebbles
that you bring from the river.

I am blind as a cave fish.
You can only watch shuddering
whenever I suck the whiteness,
whenever my hurricane eyes
rush open under your skin.

Sebastian

With a sardonic forbearance
in eyes that had seen too much
he stands in a Brooklyn butcher shop
on the floor of my memory.

Hands smelling of homemade wine
he walked his tiny rose garden
with the years in Castelvetrano
still whirring in his ears.

We knew less and less of him—we were only
the motes at the edge of his gaze
when he greeted us at the shop
in his white blood-stained apron.

And when the *capo* entered wanting to be paid
my grandfather's eyes blinked once before
he scowled and pointed to the empty meat hook
hanging inside the freezer's open door.

He knew less and less of us
when he walked his New World wilderness
with the aroma in his nostrils
of sawdust and animal blood.

The Apparition Comes

It was the year the dogwood forgot to bloom,
the year its palsied gray branch finally fell,
the year a pandemic blew hooded spirits
of plague doctors through our dreams.

Yet it was a relief the apocalypse
had finally come, we were so exhausted
we swanned into our beds to sleep
in the drumbeat of our own dread.

And woke to haunt the halls
of a quarantine so long and still
it dizzied us while it set us free.

We refused money and shoes
and lit oil lamps so we could
read the sibyl's leaves.

Then chalked her unforgiving words
in black on the walls, we were
so giddy we fasted and whispered
during insane days, wretched nights.

And when it ended we found our way back
without appetite through the darkness
finally knowing the entire truth of our lives.

Anonymous Woman

Now that I've embraced
the petrifications of the body.
Now that I am somewhere
above and below.

Now that I've sung the final
duet with my soul
I ask myself what was it
I was meant to know.

I hear the echo of an infant's laugh
when I hopscotch through the night
or do one perfect pirouette
holding the moon in my arms.

And I keep drifting toward the future
here at life's wistful edge—
what I know stands out in the open field
with a sunflower's lowered head.

Wind

It came beckoning, nodding
in cap and bells, it came
strumming its funny lips.

It played torch songs on a cello
carved of glass and satinwood,
its voice leaping like a gazelle.

It came holding out its hand
to partner you for the tarantella
or an erotic minuet.

You let it sing to you, you let it
sweep you into the sequined shawl
of ten thousand flowers and leaves.

You let it lull you with
an executioner's stony tick,
with old rhapsodies of brine and ash.

Swans

The swans rise like ghosts
breast to breast from the water.
Then slowly they descend
and drift with shy authority
out over the moonlit deeps.
I have taken my vows.
Quietly I have watched them
strip and eat the brittle
brilliant leaves of willows,
heard their hoarse whispers
reel off through the lagoon
like sibilant winds. I have
felt the ardent vibration
of their wings humming
as they take to the air
trailing the ephemera of stars.
They fly high and fast
and let the souls of poets
pass forever through them
like strong bright knives.

Kindness

With the gravity of exiles
passengers keep boarding the bus
that takes you all the way through the city
while the form taking shape in your mind
deepens as each new passenger arrives.

The form knows your ways,
she observes your every hesitation,
the full breadth of your pain
for now like others in the world
you have suffered.

At last you speak to her—you humbly ask
for absolution when the bus reaches the park.
And tenderly she forgives you at the very last stop
as the day darkens, as you follow her
on the forgotten journey of kindness.

Icicles

Crisp silhouettes of watery silver light.
Sleek harbingers of frozen myth.
We try but never quite catch you
in the act of becoming what you are.

Translucent tusks slung downward
passing through our enigmatic lives
encased in tapers of glass,
inverted in mysterious obelisks.

We want to keep you in our posthumous tableaus,
savor the eloquence of your crystalline might.
Your hard-won columns of clarity ticking
or dripping as the atmosphere allows.

Because you successfully resist rainbows.
You have nothing to confess or deny.
Alone you stand for something more than
honor and purity, imagination and delight.

Mask

The avalanche rolls over me
and sweeps aside my mask.
Thank you, snow, wind, and ice—
you leave no echoes in the mind.

And thank you for this new expression
now that the mask is gone.
I wore it for so long it seemed
to grow into my face.

Each day I looked into the mirror
and drew the mask back on.
With a pencil I simply followed
the map of deepening lines.

Now the deadline has come
for masquerades never last.
So a toast to the new life
without mirrors, without masks.

Winter Walk

I hear the clock tick and see
my dog's tongue flicker with
the itch of unspoken words.

The smoke of libido no longer
hovers over my path but I am
aware of the urgency of thunder.

This is no message in a bottle—
my name is already incised deep
into a stone out in the chapel yard.

And even the statues inside the church
where I once kneeled and prayed
hold back their replies.

Lot's Wife

He had said not to look back
one last time at that city
yet it had pulled and pulled at her.

He had said to abandon her memories
yet they kept whispering
like autumn rain on the veranda.

How could she bring herself to believe
that the voices inside her house would
empty their echoes forever into the dark?

Or forget how the moonbeams
whitening her smooth tiled floors
could soothe the pains of love.

She had known beauty in that city—
to simply walk down the tree-lined streets
was to meet her own soul.

Yet she had done what he said—
sheeted the mirrors, covered the lamps
and followed him out past the city walls.

But the sound of the key turning one last time
in the lock of the front door had followed her
and she felt the slow rotation of her body

leaning back once more into the arms of that city
although the burning snow now blinded her
wildly stinging her knees, lips, eyes.

Magdalene

The moon's bright empty death mask
closes its eyes at dawn,
then cracks and shatters.

I open the gate and the wind
comes along like a blind man
leaning on me, tapping
a quick, anxious cane.

We reel through narrow, crooked streets.
The city is large and ruined.
There is feeling in every part of it.

When I approach the tomb
the white shadows of my thoughts
begin to moan and whisper
like a flock of dreaming doves.
My cloak slides and shifts.
I lift it over my mouth.

There is the shock of music.
I raise my numb arm
to rub my burning eye.
I turn.

The Waiting

On her wall
the dream condensing
into shadow.

There was a voice
lightly spraying
the silence.

The hushed pulse
of what must
have been words.

She had kept
her eyes open
and lifted her hand.

The wonder
coiling inside her
as it delivered light.

Night or day
the unstoppable growth
of radiance.

She would wake
to the faint beating
of a moth's wing.

Then the slow
bubbling turn
of head and spine.

And December
when the waiting
was everything.

Interview with Mary

How do you feel now?
Wintry but alive. Like a leopard
leaving tracks in the snow.

How do you spend your time?
I am waiting in the silence of statues.

What are you waiting for?
A wind to rise like the blue breath of God.

What do you see?
Shadows scattering at dusk.
A wave perpetually breaking.
Impenetrable darkness.

When do you sleep?
When the light leaves my fingertips.

What do you dream of?
A line of blackbirds vanishing into the clouds.
A row of women wearing the garments of dead
leaves.

What is it that you want?
I want a path to open.
I want the contours of my life
to become a landscape in white jade.

Pilgrim Journey

Torn sandals. Numb toes.
Patched robe. Hair a dusty wreath.
I pause to rest beneath a cinnamon tree
with only the wing beats of my thoughts.

Sing me a childhood song for sleep
and I will keep it like a sea-worn shell.
The catastrophes of love no longer speak to me.
The cicadas tell me what I need to know.

Walk with me to the sacred mountain.
Spin the prayer wheel to banish fear.
The clouds will not stop opening.
The path will never disappear.

Bacchus Sees Ariadne

He felt as he watched her nude
and penetrable sleep the slow story
of desire woven through her dreams,
flesh pressing flesh—the warm glowing
coals of her imagination, her head
bent back and on her breath
the scent of apples and in the depths
behind her closed eyes the quiet
moving shadow play of memory—
flesh pressing flesh, her exposed
graceful throat, the fable of her
release imprinted in her abandonment,
her uncovered breasts rising and falling
under the rush of moonlit clouds,
her arm thrust carelessly over her brow,
the spaces surrounding her body
shimmering like charmed diamonds,
like the wedding crown he would set in her hair
and later place among the stars.

Daphne Afterward

Redemption yes, but not
a spiritual mission, escape
yes, into the soul of breeze.
Sometimes I stood up straight
on rooted tiptoe to gaze
beyond the tips of sun-crazed
leaves chanting *no not you
or you or you,* not ever
would I live in the grip
of a raking passion.

So if you had climbed, stroked,
split me, I would not have
changed and if you had come
to bury treasure underneath
my trunk I would have thrown back
my head and laughed as I did
stepping out of the tree,
my arms reaching forward
to let the shadows of my hands
release the shadows of the leaves.

Memoir: Philippa Chaucer

In the house of John of Gaunt
I sewed silver buttons on scarlet cloth.
In the house of the Queen
I embroidered a coverlet
of white, sleepy women
arching their long necks
above the bodies of swans.

In the house of my husband
I knitted heavy garments
for the Queen's funeral,
my quick fingers fragrant
with the scent of black wool.

I was the wife of a writer
with strong, shapely hands.
I wanted to paint portraits
and looked into the mirror
to copy my face
but the glass went dark.

Nights when I could not sleep
I ran to the river
and watched the silent swans.

I had two children,
hairnets stitched with almondine,
and a carved satinwood bed.

Now I doze in the sun
and clasp mute white hands
unmarked
like the Queen's swans.

Ophelia

It wasn't easy living in his imagination,
the obsessions tiered like altar lights.

Oh, she tried not to stare whenever she
tiptoed past the skull racks in his dreams.

There were times when she saw him happy
but even his gaiety made her shiver.

He was a strange man given to sudden screaming—
some would have said he was a fiend.

Why did she need him, why did she ever
enter his dark, dry kingdom?

Why did she cruise the orchard like a moody crow
craving the skins of black apples?

Shelley's Heart

Taking the blue satin blood pump
that somehow refused to burn
from the scattering flames,
they proudly gave it to her as if
it were an impossibly lavish gift.

No one had ever handed her
a heart before and she stared
for a moment in sad amazement
until her own spangled blood
began to plunge and spin.

Later in England she swathed it
in brocaded cloth and locked it
like a globe of secret thunder
deep inside her desk.

She did not exactly forget it.
Whenever it rained she imagined
that the heart would shudder
and begin helplessly to drum
like a broken, hungry tambourine.

Like her own heart the night
she rushed from a moonlit carriage
in Pisa and stood stone white
at Byron's door, asking over and over,
"Do you know anything about Shelley?"

Piranesi at the Tomb of Cecilia Metella

Munching rice. Smelling snow.
The cool midnight air. The dream alive
and moving in the muscles of his face.

He would raise her ghost from the ruins
with his pen his breath, he would find his way
through the lines of broken walls.

This world of darkness and shadow
was his own—the erosion of everything
into swaying forms now black

now white now gray that come
filing toward him shifting as they go
into enigmatic masses of stone.

Transparencies of the moonlit clouds.
A pulsating mind now frost
now ash now the sudden gaze

of an imagined figure standing alone
at the center of the tomb—
the shape and size of his own despair

or his own vision of the sublime
mirrored in the ardent stare of a husband
still standing watch over her

yet she had escaped there down the hill
past the row of parasol pines or else
she was here on the Appian Way

her voice her every gesture now blurred
now erased now remade in the taut
mystical balance of these stones, these lines.

The Old World

In honor of your mutilations
from a mother's love and anger.
In honor of the Slavic village
where her father entered her bed.

In honor of the blue scar on her wrist
that she wore like a bracelet.
In honor of your insistence
I not walk too close behind you.

In honor of the Old World
of stifled whispers, muffled fears.
In honor of the burnt tundra
of an immigrant's hidden life.

I offer you the isolate blaze
of this one red poppy.
The black blood drop at its center.
Its wounded yearning for the light.

Daybook: Leonard Woolf

March 28, 1941

The fever of your dream broke at midnight.
You rose and lifted your face to the window,
watching the moon's delirium thicken
in its windy pool of paraffin. All night,
neither sleeping nor waking
you sank in the swift undertow of memories
breaking in waves of sudden light.
At dawn the impassioned tide withdrew,
trailing only a hollow moon, starved white
and patterned with open wounds
like a frail sand dollar.

All winter you have dreamed of this morning.
All your life you have scanned
the enormous silence of this morning
holding it like the lit taper
of a guttering star high
in the dark cave of your body.

Raising your slender arms
through a mantle of white wool,
you cross the garden's memory of roses
whose dazed faces reproach you
with a confusion of questions
that have gone wild and over bloomed.

Now with the reckless wind daring you,
with a new light lifting you forward,
you prepare your pockets
with a conspiracy of stones
and step into the one vision
you will never describe:
how in the piquant daylight
you fed your beautiful body
to the blue mouths of the river
cool and whispering.

Oliver in Sutri

I crouch in the forest of Sutri,
a book in my feverish hands
under stars of crushed diamond and pearl.

The dreams of my life are diamond and pearl
but I cling to the hiss of this body,
this brown parchment leaf.

He's sly, the old priest in Sutri.
When he brings me food in the evening
he watches me with glittering eyes.

I crouch in the forest of Sutri.
The dry leaves whir like castanets.
Who can stop me? I read word after word.

Jonah

Nights kneading him into reverie.
Cave pearls gleaming from the edge
of a huge rose-lit mouth.

Seafloors whirling their fields of grass.
Fish passing like monks in meditation.

To be mastered by this gray and purple mist.
By a gate of white knives slamming shut.
To exist within a tunnel of thunder.

To stand alone waiting
inside the shape of his own death.

Yet he had wanted to come all the way down
into these cool mystic depths.
To grasp the entire sea by mouthfuls.

He had wanted to breathe through blackened gills.
To wound himself with water.

Then rise slowly to the surface
and be smoke under the open sky.

Thoreau

It was better he was homely and lived alone
roaming the visions of an owl,
measuring the skeleton of a raccoon.

His mind was what he quarried
on midnight saunters through the woods
under a veined marble moon.

His walking stick was notched, his pencils crafted,
his desk built on a slant—so much the better
he was chaste and could save his love for the clouds.

He had taken the exact dimensions of his shadow,
kept disenchantments at the edge
of his life like weeds in a pond.

He watched as wind brocaded the water
and knew the right moment to raise the frame
of his house was when the snow swirled.

He was cheerful on his final day when he said
Now comes good sailing and he smiled
when he felt the water go over his eyes.

Dear Natalia

I should have accepted your invitation,
climbed all the way up the stairway
of your apartment house in Rome.

You would have offered me tea
and leaned back pensively to listen
with your chin resting on your wrist.

I would have asked to see your poems
but you would only have shrugged—
non ci importa, you might have said

as if they had been no more than
momentary lights that once rippled
in an ancient midnight tide.

There with your hair cut so short,
your thoughts already on the road
to the afterlife of the city.

For Natalia Ginzburg

Self-portrait

I woke in the twilight of childhood
musing like a carillon.

I woke dreaming of the fireflies
still winking at me.

I woke with my eyes and lips still closed,
my trust and belief still whole.

I woke exiled from every fear,
every memory of evil and pain.

I woke rushing toward redemption
with the speed of a hummingbird.

I woke swathed in a holy prayer shawl
surrounded by towers of books.

I woke with the bowed head of a nun
preparing to kneel at the altar.

I woke like an émigré riding the cloud
that would take me back to my homeland.

ABOUT THE AUTHOR

Rita Signorelli-Pappas's poems have been published in *Poetry, Shenandoah, Southwest Review, Prairie Schooner, The Literary Review, Poet Lore, The Women's Review of Books, Southern Poetry Review, Notre Dame Review,* and other publications, as well as in the online publications *Poetry Daily* and *Verse Daily*. She is a regular poetry reviewer for *World Literature Today,* and her fiction has appeared in *Helicon Nine, Italian Americana, Helicon Nine, Farmer's Market, Crosscurrents,* and *VIA*. Her short story, "Spirit Dreams" was nominated for a Pushcart Prize, and another received the fiction award in *Italian Americana*. Her two previous collections of poetry, *Satyr's Wife* (2010) and *Labyrinth* (2019), were both published by Serving House Books.

www.ingramcontent.com/pod-product-compliance
Lightning Source LLC
Chambersburg PA
CBHW060541080526
44586CB00012B/809